D1785604

GRATITUDE
JOURNAL

Copyright © 2016 Brenda Nathan

All rights reserved.

*Extracts from the Authorized Version of the Bible
(The King James Bible), the rights in which are vested
in the Crown, are reproduced by permission of the
Crown's Patentee, Cambridge University Press.*

Gratitude

Gratitude is a feeling of appreciation for what one has. It is a feeling of thankfulness for the blessings we have received.

There is an exercise at the beginning of this journal to complete before starting your daily record of gratitude.

By keeping a record of your gratitude in a journal, you will store positive energy, gain clarity in your life, and have greater control of your thoughts and emotions.

Each day, write down three to five things that you are grateful for in this journal and turn your ordinary moments into blessings.

O give thanks unto the LORD, for he is good:
for his mercy endureth for ever.

— Psalm 107:1, KJV

People I am *Grateful* for

_____

_____

_____

_____

_____

_____

_____

Top 10 memorable events in my life that I am *Grateful* for:

1. _____

2. _____

3. _____

4. _____

5. _____

6. _____

7. _____

8. _____

9. _____

10. _____

People I have made a difference to and am *Grateful* for having had this opportunity:

Top 10 memorable events in my life that I am *Grateful* for:

1.
2.
3.
4.
5.
6.
7.
8.
9.
10.

Things I have now which I am *Grateful* for:

_____

_____

_____

_____

_____

_____

_____

Top 10 teachable moments from my past that I am now *Grateful* for:

1. _____

2. _____

3. _____

4. _____

5. _____

6. _____

7. _____

8. _____

9. _____

10. _____

Day: _____ *Date:* ____ / ____ / ____

Today I am *Grateful* for _____

_____

_____

_____

_____

_____

_____

And the angel said unto them, Fear not: for, behold, I bring you good tidings of great joy, which shall be to all people. Luke 2:10, KJV

Day: _____ *Date:* ____ / ____ / ____

Today I am *Grateful* for _____

_____

_____

_____

_____

_____

_____

Day: _____ *Date:* ____ / ____ / ____

Today I am *Grateful* for _____

_____

_____

_____

_____

_____

_____

When they saw the star, they rejoiced with exceeding great joy. Matthew 2:10, KJV

Day: _____ *Date:* ____ / ____ / ____

Today I am *Grateful* for _____

_____

_____

_____

_____

_____

_____

Day: _____ *Date:* _____ / _____ / _____

Today I am *Grateful* for _____

_____

_____

_____

_____

_____

_____

Therefore the Lord himself shall give you a sign; Behold, a virgin shall conceive, and bear a son, and shall call his name Immanuel. Isaiah 7:14, KJV

Day: _____ *Date:* _____ / _____ / _____

Today I am *Grateful* for _____

_____

_____

_____

_____

_____

_____

Day: _____ *Date:* ____/ ____/ ____

Today I am *Grateful* for _____

_____

_____

_____

_____

_____

_____

Glory to God in the highest, and on earth peace, good will toward men. Luke 2:14, KJV

Day: _____ *Date:* ____/ ____/ ____

Today I am *Grateful* for _____

_____

_____

_____

_____

_____

_____

Day: _____ *Date:* ____ / ____ / ____

Today I am *Grateful* for _____

_____

_____

_____

_____

_____

_____

Now the God of hope fill you with all joy and peace in believing, that ye may abound in hope, through the power of the Holy Ghost. Romans 15:13, KJV

Day: _____ *Date:* ____ / ____ / ____

Today I am *Grateful* for _____

_____

_____

_____

_____

_____

_____

Day: _____ *Date:* ____/____/____

Today I am *Grateful* for _____

_____

_____

_____

_____

_____

_____

Thanks be unto God for his unspeakable gift. 2 Corinthians 9:15, KJV

Day: _____ *Date:* ____/____/____

Today I am *Grateful* for _____

_____

_____

_____

_____

_____

Day: _____ *Date:* ____ / ____ / ____

Today I am *Grateful* for _____

_____

_____

_____

_____

_____

_____

This is the day which the LORD hath made; we will rejoice and be glad in it.
Psalm 118:24, KJV

Day: _____ *Date:* ____ / ____ / ____

Today I am *Grateful* for _____

_____

_____

_____

_____

_____

_____

Day: _____ *Date:* ____ / ____ / ____

Today I am *Grateful* for _____

_____

_____

_____

_____

_____

_____

Every good gift and every perfect gift is from above, and cometh down from the Father of lights, with whom is no variableness, neither shadow of turning. James 1:17, KJV

Day: _____ *Date:* ____ / ____ / ____

Today I am *Grateful* for _____

_____

_____

_____

_____

_____

_____

Day: _____ *Date:* _____ / _____ / _____

Today I am *Grateful* for _____

_____

_____

_____

_____

_____

_____

In every thing give thanks: for this is the will of God in Christ Jesus concerning you. 1 Thessalonians 5:18, KJV

Day: _____ *Date:* _____ / _____ / _____

Today I am *Grateful* for _____

_____

_____

_____

_____

_____

Day: _____ *Date:* ____/____/____

Today I am *Grateful* for _____

_____
_____
_____
_____
_____
_____

And whatsoever ye do in word or deed, do all in the name of the Lord Jesus, giving thanks to God and the Father by him.   Colossians 3:17, KJV

Day: _____ *Date:* ____/____/____

Today I am *Grateful* for _____

_____
_____
_____
_____
_____

Day: _____ *Date:* ____ / ____ / ____

Today I am *Grateful* for _____

_____

_____

_____

_____

_____

_____

Giving thanks always for all things unto God and the Father in the name of our Lord
Jesus Christ; Ephesians 5:20, KJV

Day: _____ *Date:* ____ / ____ / ____

Today I am *Grateful* for _____

_____

_____

_____

_____

_____

_____

Day: _____ *Date:* ____ / ____ / ____

Today I am *Grateful* for _____

_____

_____

_____

_____

_____

_____

Wherefore we receiving a kingdom which cannot be moved, let us have grace, whereby we may serve God acceptably with reverence and godly fear: Hebrews 12:28, KJV

Day: _____ *Date:* ____ / ____ / ____

Today I am *Grateful* for _____

_____

_____

_____

_____

_____

_____

Day: _____ *Date:* ____ / ____ / ____

Today I am *Grateful* for _____

_____

_____

_____

_____

_____

_____

_____

*And let the peace of God rule in your hearts, to the which also ye are called in one body;
and be ye thankful. Colossians 3:15, KJV*

Day: _____ *Date:* ____ / ____ / ____

Today I am *Grateful* for _____

_____

_____

_____

_____

_____

_____

Day: _____ *Date:* ____/ ____/ ____

Today I am *Grateful* for _____

_____

_____

_____

_____

_____

_____

And we know that all things work together for good to them that love God, to them who are the called according to his purpose. Romans 8:28, KJV

Day: _____ *Date:* ____/ ____/ ____

Today I am *Grateful* for _____

_____

_____

_____

_____

_____

_____

Day: _____ *Date:* _____ / _____ / _____

Today I am *Grateful* for _____

_____

_____

_____

_____

_____

_____

For where your treasure is, there will your heart be also. Matthew 6:21, KJV

Day: _____ *Date:* _____ / _____ / _____

Today I am *Grateful* for _____

_____

_____

_____

_____

_____

_____

Day: _____ *Date:* ____/ ____/ ____

Today I am *Grateful* for _____

_____

_____

_____

_____

_____

_____

Continue in prayer, and watch in the same with thanksgiving; Colossians 4:2, KJV

Day: _____ *Date:* ____/ ____/ ____

Today I am *Grateful* for _____

_____

_____

_____

_____

_____

Day: _____ *Date:* ____ / ____ / ____

Today I am *Grateful* for _____

_____

_____

_____

_____

_____

_____

We accept it always, and in all places, most noble Felix, with all thankfulness.
Acts 24:3, KJV

Day: _____ *Date:* ____ / ____ / ____

Today I am *Grateful* for _____

_____

_____

_____

_____

_____

_____

Day: _____ *Date:* ____ / ____ / ____

Today I am *Grateful* for _____

_____

_____

_____

_____

_____

_____

But by the grace of God I am what I am: and his grace which was bestowed upon me was not in vain; but I laboured more abundantly than they all: yet not I, but the grace of God which was with me. 1 Corinthians 15:10, KJV

Day: _____ *Date:* ____ / ____ / ____

Today I am *Grateful* for _____

_____

_____

_____

_____

_____

_____

Day: _____ *Date:* _____ / _____ / _____

Today I am *Grateful* for _____

_____

_____

_____

_____

_____

Then they took away the stone from the place where the dead was laid. And Jesus lifted up his eyes, and said, Father, I thank thee that thou hast heard me. John 11:41, KJV

Day: _____ *Date:* _____ / _____ / _____

Today I am *Grateful* for _____

_____

_____

_____

_____

_____

Day: _____ *Date:* _____ / _____ / _____

Today I am *Grateful* for _____

_____

_____

_____

_____

_____

_____

*By him therefore let us offer the sacrifice of praise to God continually, that is, the fruit of
our lips giving thanks to his name. Hebrews 13:15, KJV*

Day: _____ *Date:* _____ / _____ / _____

Today I am *Grateful* for _____

_____

_____

_____

_____

_____

Day: _____ *Date:* ____ / ____ / ____

Today I am *Grateful* for _____

_____

_____

_____

_____

_____

_____

Cease not to give thanks for you, making mention of you in my prayers;
Ephesians 1:16, KJV

Day: _____ *Date:* ____ / ____ / ____

Today I am *Grateful* for _____

_____

_____

_____

_____

_____

_____

Day: _____ *Date:* ____/ ____/ ____

Today I am *Grateful* for _____

_____

_____

_____

_____

_____

_____

We love him, because he first loved us. 1 John 4:19, KJV

Day: _____ *Date:* ____/ ____/ ____

Today I am *Grateful* for _____

_____

_____

_____

_____

_____

Day: _____ *Date:* ____ / ____ / ____

Today I am *Grateful* for _____

_____

_____

_____

_____

_____

Let the word of Christ dwell in you richly in all wisdom; teaching and admonishing one another in psalms and hymns and spiritual songs, singing with grace in your hearts to the Lord. Colossians 3:16, KJV

Day: _____ *Date:* ____ / ____ / ____

Today I am *Grateful* for _____

_____

_____

_____

_____

_____

Day: _____ *Date:* ____/ ____/ ____

Today I am *Grateful* for _____

_____

_____

_____

_____

_____

_____

I exhort therefore, that, first of all, supplications, prayers, intercessions, and giving of thanks, be made for all men; 1 Timothy 2:1, KJV

Day: _____ *Date:* ____/ ____/ ____

Today I am *Grateful* for _____

_____

_____

_____

_____

_____

Day: _____ *Date:* ____ / ____ / ____

Today I am *Grateful* for _____

_____

_____

_____

_____

_____

_____

O give thanks unto the LORD; call upon his name: make known his deeds among the people. Psalm 105:1, KJV

Day: _____ *Date:* ____ / ____ / ____

Today I am *Grateful* for _____

_____

_____

_____

_____

_____

_____

Day: _____ *Date:* ____ / ____ / ____

Today I am *Grateful* for _____

_____

_____

_____

_____

_____

They are new every morning: great is thy faithfulness. Lamentations 3:23, KJV

Day: _____ *Date:* ____ / ____ / ____

Today I am *Grateful* for _____

_____

_____

_____

_____

_____

Day: _____ *Date:* ____ / ____ / ____

Today I am *Grateful* for _____

_____

_____

_____

_____

_____

_____

A Psalm or Song for the sabbath day. It is a good thing to give thanks unto the LORD, and to sing praises unto thy name, O most High: Psalm 92:1, KJV

Day: _____ *Date:* ____ / ____ / ____

Today I am *Grateful* for _____

_____

_____

_____

_____

_____

_____

Day: _____ *Date:* ____/ ____/ ____

Today I am *Grateful* for _____

_____

_____

_____

_____

_____

_____

I can do all things through Christ which strengtheneth me. Philippians 4:13, KJV

Day: _____ *Date:* ____/ ____/ ____

Today I am *Grateful* for _____

_____

_____

_____

_____

_____

Day: _____ *Date:* ____ / ____ / ____

Today I am *Grateful* for _____

_____

_____

_____

_____

_____

_____

Now thanks be unto God, which always causeth us to triumph in Christ, and maketh manifest the savour of his knowledge by us in every place. 2 Corinthians 2:14, KJV

Day: _____ *Date:* ____ / ____ / ____

Today I am *Grateful* for _____

_____

_____

_____

_____

_____

_____

Day: _____ *Date:* ____/ ____/ ____

Today I am *Grateful* for _____

_____

_____

_____

_____

_____

_____

The LORD is my strength and my shield; my heart trusted in him, and I am helped: therefore my heart greatly rejoiceth; and with my song will I praise him. Psalm 28:7, KJV

Day: _____ *Date:* ____/ ____/ ____

Today I am *Grateful* for _____

_____

_____

_____

_____

_____

_____

Day: _____ *Date:* ____ / ____ / ____

Today I am *Grateful* for _____

_____

_____

_____

_____

_____

_____

Offer unto God thanksgiving; and pay thy vows unto the most High: Psalm 50:14, KJV

Day: _____ *Date:* ____ / ____ / ____

Today I am *Grateful* for _____

_____

_____

_____

_____

_____

_____

Day: _____ *Date:* ____ / ____ / ____

Today I am *Grateful* for _____

_____

_____

_____

_____

_____

_____

Come unto me, all ye that labour and are heavy laden, and I will give you rest.
Matthew 11:28, KJV

Day: _____ *Date:* ____ / ____ / ____

Today I am *Grateful* for _____

_____

_____

_____

_____

_____

Day: _____ *Date:* ____ / ____ / ____

Today I am *Grateful* for _____

_____

_____

_____

_____

_____

_____

Bless the LORD, O my soul, and forget not all his benefits: Psalm 103:2, KJV

Day: _____ *Date:* ____ / ____ / ____

Today I am *Grateful* for _____

_____

_____

_____

_____

_____

_____

Day: _____ *Date:* _____ / _____ / _____

Today I am *Grateful* for _____

_____

_____

_____

_____

_____

_____

Fear thou not; for I am with thee: be not dismayed; for I am thy God: I will strengthen thee;
yea, I will help thee; yea, I will uphold thee with the right hand of my righteousness.
Isaiah 41:10, KJV

Day: _____ *Date:* _____ / _____ / _____

Today I am *Grateful* for _____

_____

_____

_____

_____

_____

Day: _____ *Date:* ____ / ____ / ____

Today I am *Grateful* for _____

_____

_____

_____

_____

_____

_____

I will praise the LORD according to his righteousness: and will sing praise to the name of the LORD most high. Psalm 7:17, KJV

Day: _____ *Date:* ____ / ____ / ____

Today I am *Grateful* for _____

_____

_____

_____

_____

_____

Day: _____ *Date:* ____ / ____ / ____

Today I am *Grateful* for _____

_____

_____

_____

_____

_____

_____

_____

*Remember, O LORD, thy tender mercies and thy lovingkindnesses; for they have
been ever of old. Psalm 25:6, KJV*

Day: _____ *Date:* ____ / ____ / ____

Today I am *Grateful* for _____

_____

_____

_____

_____

_____

_____

Day: _____ *Date:* ____ / ____ / ____

Today I am *Grateful* for _____

_____

_____

_____

_____

_____

_____

For God so loved the world, that he gave his only begotten Son, that whosoever believeth in him should not perish, but have everlasting life. John 3:16, KJV

Day: _____ *Date:* ____ / ____ / ____

Today I am *Grateful* for _____

_____

_____

_____

_____

_____

_____

Day: _____ *Date:* ____ / ____ / ____

Today I am *Grateful* for _____

_____

_____

_____

_____

_____

The Lord knoweth how to deliver the godly out of temptations, and to reserve the unjust unto the day of judgment to be punished: 2 Peter 2:9, KJV

Day: _____ *Date:* ____ / ____ / ____

Today I am *Grateful* for _____

_____

_____

_____

_____

_____

Day: _____ *Date:* ____/ ____/ ____

Today I am *Grateful* for _____

_____

_____

_____

_____

_____

_____

Greater love hath no man than this, that a man lay down his life for his friends.
John 15:13, KJV

Day: _____ *Date:* ____/ ____/ ____

Today I am *Grateful* for _____

_____

_____

_____

_____

_____

_____

Day: _____ *Date:* ____ / ____ / ____

Today I am *Grateful* for _____

_____

_____

_____

_____

_____

_____

Better is the sight of the eyes than the wandering of the desire: this is also vanity and vexation of spirit. Ecclesiastes 6:9, KJV

Day: _____ *Date:* ____ / ____ / ____

Today I am *Grateful* for _____

_____

_____

_____

_____

_____

_____

Day: _____ *Date:* ____ / ____ / ____

Today I am *Grateful* for _____

_____

_____

_____

_____

_____

_____

Say unto God, How terrible art thou in thy works! through the greatness of thy power shall thine enemies submit themselves unto thee. Psalm 66:3, KJV

Day: _____ *Date:* ____ / ____ / ____

Today I am *Grateful* for _____

_____

_____

_____

_____

_____

Day: _____ *Date:* ____/____/____

Today I am *Grateful* for _____

_____

_____

_____

_____

_____

_____

A Psalm of David. The LORD is my shepherd; I shall not want. Psalm 23:1, KJV

Day: _____ *Date:* ____/____/____

Today I am *Grateful* for _____

_____

_____

_____

_____

_____

Day: _____ *Date:* ____ / ____ / ____

Today I am *Grateful* for _____

_____

_____

_____

_____

_____

_____

For the people shall dwell in Zion at Jerusalem: thou shalt weep no more: he will be very gracious unto thee at the voice of thy cry; when he shall hear it, he will answer thee.
Isaiah 30:19, KJV

Day: _____ *Date:* ____ / ____ / ____

Today I am *Grateful* for _____

_____

_____

_____

_____

_____

Day: _____ *Date:* ____/ ____/ ____

Today I am *Grateful* for _____

_____

_____

_____

_____

_____

_____

Give thanks unto the LORD, call upon his name, make known his deeds among the people. 1 Chronicles 16:8, KJV

Day: _____ *Date:* ____/ ____/ ____

Today I am *Grateful* for _____

_____

_____

_____

_____

_____

Day: _____ *Date:* ____ / ____ / ____

Today I am *Grateful* for _____

_____

_____

_____

_____

_____

_____

Thou art worthy, O Lord, to receive glory and honour and power: for thou hast created all things, and for thy pleasure they are and were created. Revelation 4:11, KJV

Day: _____ *Date:* ____ / ____ / ____

Today I am *Grateful* for _____

_____

_____

_____

_____

_____

_____

Day: _____ *Date:* ____/____/____

Today I am *Grateful* for _____

_____

_____

_____

_____

_____

_____

Then Jesus said unto them, Verily, verily, I say unto you, Except ye eat the flesh of the Son of man, and drink his blood, ye have no life in you. John 6:53, KJV

Day: _____ *Date:* ____/____/____

Today I am *Grateful* for _____

_____

_____

_____

_____

_____

_____

Day: _____ *Date:* ____ / ____ / ____

Today I am *Grateful* for _____

_____

_____

_____

_____

_____

_____

But whosoever drinketh of the water that I shall give him shall never thirst; but the water that I shall give him shall be in him a well of water springing up into everlasting life.
John 4:14, KJV

Day: _____ *Date:* ____ / ____ / ____

Today I am *Grateful* for _____

_____

_____

_____

_____

_____

_____

Day: _____ *Date:* ____/ ____/ ____

Today I am *Grateful* for _____

_____

_____

_____

_____

_____

_____

But the fruit of the Spirit is love, joy, peace, longsuffering, gentleness, goodness, faith,
Galatians 5:22, KJV

Day: _____ *Date:* ____/ ____/ ____

Today I am *Grateful* for _____

_____

_____

_____

_____

_____

Day: _____ *Date:* ____ / ____ / ____

Today I am *Grateful* for _____

_____

_____

_____

_____

_____

_____

And he leaping up stood, and walked, and entered with them into the temple, walking, and leaping, and praising God. Acts 3:8, KJV

Day: _____ *Date:* ____ / ____ / ____

Today I am *Grateful* for _____

_____

_____

_____

_____

_____

_____

Day: _____ *Date:* _____ / _____ / _____

Today I am *Grateful* for _____

_____

_____

_____

_____

_____

_____

This book of the law shall not depart out of thy mouth; but thou shalt meditate therein day and night, that thou mayest observe to do according to all that is written therein: for then thou shalt make thy way prosperous, and then thou shalt have good success.
Joshua 1:8, KJV

Day: _____ *Date:* _____ / _____ / _____

Today I am *Grateful* for _____

_____

_____

_____

_____

_____

Day: _____ *Date:* _____ / _____ / _____

Today I am *Grateful* for _____

_____

_____

_____

_____

_____

_____

Jesus saith unto him, I am the way, the truth, and the life: no man cometh unto the Father, but by me. John 14:6, KJV

Day: _____ *Date:* _____ / _____ / _____

Today I am *Grateful* for _____

_____

_____

_____

_____

_____

_____

Day: _____ *Date:* ____/ ____/ ____

Today I am *Grateful* for _____

_____

_____

_____

_____

_____

_____

The thief cometh not, but for to steal, and to kill, and to destroy: I am come that they might have life, and that they might have it more abundantly. John 10:10, KJV

Day: _____ *Date:* ____/ ____/ ____

Today I am *Grateful* for _____

_____

_____

_____

_____

_____

Day: _____ *Date:* ____ / ____ / ____

Today I am *Grateful* for _____

_____

_____

_____

_____

_____

_____

Let no man therefore judge you in meat, or in drink, or in respect of an holyday, or of the new moon, or of the sabbath days: Colossians 2:16, KJV

Day: _____ *Date:* ____ / ____ / ____

Today I am *Grateful* for _____

_____

_____

_____

_____

_____

_____

Day: _____ *Date:* ____ / ____ / ____

Today I am *Grateful* for _____

_____

_____

_____

_____

_____

_____

And being made perfect, he became the author of eternal salvation unto all them that obey him; Hebrews 5:9, KJV

Day: _____ *Date:* ____ / ____ / ____

Today I am *Grateful* for _____

_____

_____

_____

_____

_____

Day: _____ *Date:* ____ / ____ / ____

Today I am *Grateful* for _____

_____

_____

_____

_____

_____

_____

For I am not ashamed of the gospel of Christ: for it is the power of God unto salvation to every one that believeth; to the Jew first, and also to the Greek. Romans 1:16, KJV

Day: _____ *Date:* ____ / ____ / ____

Today I am *Grateful* for _____

_____

_____

_____

_____

_____

_____

Day: _____ *Date:* ____ / ____ / ____

Today I am *Grateful* for _____

_____

_____

_____

_____

_____

_____

And thou shalt have joy and gladness; and many shall rejoice at his birth.
Luke 1:14, KJV

Day: _____ *Date:* ____ / ____ / ____

Today I am *Grateful* for _____

_____

_____

_____

_____

_____

Day: _____ *Date:* ____ / ____ / ____

Today I am *Grateful* for _____

_____

_____

_____

_____

_____

_____

One man esteemeth one day above another: another esteemeth every day alike. Let every man be fully persuaded in his own mind. Romans 14:5, KJV

Day: _____ *Date:* ____ / ____ / ____

Today I am *Grateful* for _____

_____

_____

_____

_____

_____

_____

Day: _____ *Date:* ____ / ____ / ____

Today I am *Grateful* for _____

_____

_____

_____

_____

_____

_____

Now I praise you, brethren, that ye remember me in all things, and keep the ordinances, as I delivered them to you. 1 Corinthians 11:2, KJV

Day: _____ *Date:* ____ / ____ / ____

Today I am *Grateful* for _____

_____

_____

_____

_____

_____

Day: _____ *Date:* ____ / ____ / ____

Today I am *Grateful* for _____

_____

_____

_____

_____

_____

And I heard a great voice out of heaven saying, Behold, the tabernacle of God is with men, and he will dwell with them, and they shall be his people, and God himself shall be with them, and be their God. Revelation 21:3, KJV

Day: _____ *Date:* ____ / ____ / ____

Today I am *Grateful* for _____

_____

_____

_____

_____

_____

Day: _____ *Date:* ____ / ____ / ____

Today I am *Grateful* for _____

_____

_____

_____

_____

_____

_____

And God shall wipe away all tears from their eyes; and there shall be no more death, neither sorrow, nor crying, neither shall there be any more pain: for the former things are passed away. Revelation 21:4, KJV

Day: _____ *Date:* ____ / ____ / ____

Today I am *Grateful* for _____

_____

_____

_____

_____

_____

_____

Day: _____ *Date:* ____ / ____ / ____

Today I am *Grateful* for _____

_____

_____

_____

_____

_____

For in him dwelleth all the fulness of the Godhead bodily. Colossians 2:9, KJV

Day: _____ *Date:* ____ / ____ / ____

Today I am *Grateful* for _____

_____

_____

_____

_____

_____

Day: _____ *Date:* ____ / ____ / ____

Today I am *Grateful* for _____

_____

_____

_____

_____

_____

_____

To every thing there is a season, and a time to every purpose under the heaven:
Ecclesiastes 3:1, KJV

Day: _____ *Date:* ____ / ____ / ____

Today I am *Grateful* for _____

_____

_____

_____

_____

_____

Day: _____ *Date:* ____ / ____ / ____

Today I am *Grateful* for _____

_____

_____

_____

_____

_____

_____

All things are lawful unto me, but all things are not expedient: all things are lawful for me,
but I will not be brought under the power of any. 1 Corinthians 6:12, KJV

Day: _____ *Date:* ____ / ____ / ____

Today I am *Grateful* for _____

_____

_____

_____

_____

_____

_____

Day: _____ *Date:* ____ / ____ / ____

Today I am *Grateful* for _____

_____

_____

_____

_____

_____

As long as I am in the world, I am the light of the world. John 9:5, KJV

Day: _____ *Date:* ____ / ____ / ____

Today I am *Grateful* for _____

_____

_____

_____

_____

_____

Day: _____ *Date:* ____ / ____ / ____

Today I am *Grateful* for _____

_____

_____

_____

_____

_____

_____

Then spake Jesus again unto them, saying, I am the light of the world: he that followeth me shall not walk in darkness, but shall have the light of life. John 8:12, KJV

Day: _____ *Date:* ____ / ____ / ____

Today I am *Grateful* for _____

_____

_____

_____

_____

_____

_____

Day: _____ *Date:* ____/ ____/ ____

Today I am *Grateful* for _____

_____

_____

_____

_____

_____

_____

*In the last day, that great day of the feast, Jesus stood and cried, saying, If any man thirst,
let him come unto me, and drink. John 7:37, KJV*

Day: _____ *Date:* ____/ ____/ ____

Today I am *Grateful* for _____

_____

_____

_____

_____

_____

Day: _____ *Date:* ____ / ____ / ____

Today I am *Grateful* for _____

_____

_____

_____

_____

_____

_____

But rather seek ye the kingdom of God; and all these things shall be added unto you.
Luke 12:31, KJV

Day: _____ *Date:* ____ / ____ / ____

Today I am *Grateful* for _____

_____

_____

_____

_____

_____

Day: _____ *Date:* _____ / _____ / _____

Today I am *Grateful* for _____

_____

_____

_____

_____

_____

_____

But in the last days it shall come to pass, that the mountain of the house of the LORD shall be established in the top of the mountains, and it shall be exalted above the hills; and people shall flow unto it. Micah 4:1, KJV

Day: _____ *Date:* _____ / _____ / _____

Today I am *Grateful* for _____

_____

_____

_____

_____

_____

Day: _____ *Date:* _____ / _____ / _____

Today I am *Grateful* for _____

_____

_____

_____

_____

_____

_____

Then shall we know, if we follow on to know the LORD: his going forth is prepared as the morning; and he shall come unto us as the rain, as the latter and former rain unto the earth.
Hosea 6:3, KJV

Day: _____ *Date:* _____ / _____ / _____

Today I am *Grateful* for _____

_____

_____

_____

_____

_____

_____

Day: _____ *Date:* ____/____/____

Today I am *Grateful* for _____

_____

_____

_____

_____

_____

_____

Moreover the prince shall not take of the people's inheritance by oppression, to thrust them out of their possession; but he shall give his sons inheritance out of his own possession: that my people be not scattered every man from his possession. Ezekiel 46:18, KJV

Day: _____ *Date:* ____/____/____

Today I am *Grateful* for _____

_____

_____

_____

_____

_____

_____

Day: _____ *Date:* ____ / ____ / ____

Today I am *Grateful* for _____

_____

_____

_____

_____

_____

_____

For thou hast been a strength to the poor, a strength to the needy in his distress, a refuge from the storm, a shadow from the heat, when the blast of the terrible ones is as a storm against the wall. Isaiah 25:4, KJV

Day: _____ *Date:* ____ / ____ / ____

Today I am *Grateful* for _____

_____

_____

_____

_____

_____

_____

Day: _____ *Date:* ____/ ____/ ____

Today I am *Grateful* for _____

_____

_____

_____

_____

_____

_____

House and riches are the inheritance of fathers: and a prudent wife is from the LORD. Proverbs 19:14, KJV

Day: _____ *Date:* ____/ ____/ ____

Today I am *Grateful* for _____

_____

_____

_____

_____

_____

Day: _____ *Date:* ____ / ____ / ____

Today I am *Grateful* for _____

_____

_____

_____

_____

_____

_____

And she brought forth her firstborn son, and wrapped him in swaddling clothes, and laid him in a manger; because there was no room for them in the inn. Luke 2:7, KJV

Day: _____ *Date:* ____ / ____ / ____

Today I am *Grateful* for _____

_____

_____

_____

_____

_____

_____

Day: _____ *Date:* ____ / ____ / ____

Today I am *Grateful* for _____

_____

_____

_____

_____

_____

_____

And there were in the same country shepherds abiding in the field, keeping watch over their flock by night. Luke 2:8, KJV

Day: _____ *Date:* ____ / ____ / ____

Today I am *Grateful* for _____

_____

_____

_____

_____

_____

_____

Day: _____ *Date:* ____/____/____

Today I am *Grateful* for _____

_____

_____

_____

_____

_____

_____

Yea, many people and strong nations shall come to seek the LORD of hosts in Jerusalem, and to pray before the LORD. Zechariah 8:22, KJV

Day: _____ *Date:* ____/____/____

Today I am *Grateful* for _____

_____

_____

_____

_____

_____

_____

Day: _____ *Date:* ____ / ____ / ____

Today I am *Grateful* for _____

_____

_____

_____

_____

_____

Hatred stirreth up strifes: but love covereth all sins. Proverbs 10:12, KJV

Day: _____ *Date:* ____ / ____ / ____

Today I am *Grateful* for _____

_____

_____

_____

_____

_____

Day: _____ *Date:* ____ / ____ / ____

Today I am *Grateful* for _____

_____

_____

_____

_____

_____

_____

Be kindly affectioned one to another with brotherly love; in honour preferring one another;
Romans 12:10, KJV

Day: _____ *Date:* ____ / ____ / ____

Today I am *Grateful* for _____

_____

_____

_____

_____

_____

_____

Day: _____ *Date:* ____/____/____

Today I am *Grateful* for _____

_____

_____

_____

_____

_____

_____

Love worketh no ill to his neighbour: therefore love is the fulfilling of the law.
Romans 13:10, KJV

Day: _____ *Date:* ____/____/____

Today I am *Grateful* for _____

_____

_____

_____

_____

_____

_____

Day: _____ *Date:* ____ / ____ / ____

Today I am *Grateful* for _____

_____

_____

_____

_____

_____

Beloved, let us love one another: for love is of God; and every one that loveth is born of God, and knoweth God. 1 John 4:7, KJV

Day: _____ *Date:* ____ / ____ / ____

Today I am *Grateful* for _____

_____

_____

_____

_____

_____

Day: _____ *Date:* ____/____/____

Today I am *Grateful* for _____

_____

_____

_____

_____

_____

_____

He that loveth not knoweth not God; for God is love. 1 John 4:8, KJV

Day: _____ *Date:* ____/____/____

Today I am *Grateful* for _____

_____

_____

_____

_____

_____

Day: _____ *Date:* ____ / ____ / ____

Today I am *Grateful* for _____

_____

_____

_____

_____

_____

If ye love me, keep my commandments. John 14:15, KJV

Day: _____ *Date:* ____ / ____ / ____

Today I am *Grateful* for _____

_____

_____

_____

_____

_____

Day: _____ *Date:* ____/____/____

Today I am *Grateful* for _____

_____

_____

_____

_____

_____

_____

There is no fear in love; but perfect love casteth out fear: because fear hath torment. He that feareth is not made perfect in love. 1 John 4:18, KJV

Day: _____ *Date:* ____/____/____

Today I am *Grateful* for _____

_____

_____

_____

_____

_____

_____

Day: _____ *Date:* ____ / ____ / ____

Today I am *Grateful* for _____

_____

_____

_____

_____

_____

But love ye your enemies, and do good, and lend, hoping for nothing again; and your reward shall be great, and ye shall be the children of the Highest: for he is kind unto the unthankful and to the evil. Luke 6:35, KJV

Day: _____ *Date:* ____ / ____ / ____

Today I am *Grateful* for _____

_____

_____

_____

_____

_____

Day: _____ *Date:* ____ / ____ / ____

Today I am *Grateful* for _____

_____

_____

_____

_____

_____

_____

And the second is like, namely this, Thou shalt love thy neighbour as thyself. There is none other commandment greater than these. Mark 12:31, KJV

Day: _____ *Date:* ____ / ____ / ____

Today I am *Grateful* for _____

_____

_____

_____

_____

_____

Day: _____ *Date:* ___ / ___ / ___

Today I am *Grateful* for _____

_____

_____

_____

_____

_____

_____

Jesus said unto him, Thou shalt love the Lord thy God with all thy heart, and with all thy soul, and with all thy mind. Matthew 22:37, KJV

Day: _____ *Date:* ___ / ___ / ___

Today I am *Grateful* for _____

_____

_____

_____

_____

_____

Day: _____ *Date:* _____ / _____ / _____

Today I am *Grateful* for _____

_____

_____

_____

_____

_____

_____

And they, continuing daily with one accord in the temple, and breaking bread from house to house, did eat their meat with gladness and singleness of heart, Acts 2:46, KJV

Day: _____ *Date:* _____ / _____ / _____

Today I am *Grateful* for _____

_____

_____

_____

_____

_____

Day: _____ *Date:* ____ / ____ / ____

Today I am *Grateful* for _____

_____

_____

_____

_____

_____

No man can serve two masters: for either he will hate the one, and love the other; or else he will hold to the one, and despise the other. Ye cannot serve God and mammon.
Matthew 6:24, KJV

Day: _____ *Date:* ____ / ____ / ____

Today I am *Grateful* for _____

_____

_____

_____

_____

_____

Day: _____ *Date:* _____ / _____ / _____

Today I am *Grateful* for _____

_____

_____

_____

_____

_____

_____

Thou shalt not avenge, nor bear any grudge against the children of thy people, but thou shalt love thy neighbour as thyself: I am the LORD. Leviticus 19:18, KJV

Day: _____ *Date:* _____ / _____ / _____

Today I am *Grateful* for _____

_____

_____

_____

_____

_____

_____

Day: _____ *Date:* _____ / _____ / _____

Today I am *Grateful* for _____

_____

_____

_____

_____

_____

_____

And as ye would that men should do to you, do ye also to them likewise. Luke 6:31, KJV

Day: _____ *Date:* _____ / _____ / _____

Today I am *Grateful* for _____

_____

_____

_____

_____

_____

_____

Day: _____ *Date:* ____/ ____/ ____

Today I am *Grateful* for _____

_____

_____

_____

_____

_____

_____

Owe no man any thing, but to love one another: for he that loveth another hath fulfilled the law. Romans 13:8, KJV

Day: _____ *Date:* ____/ ____/ ____

Today I am *Grateful* for _____

_____

_____

_____

_____

_____

_____

Day: _____ *Date:* ____ / ____ / ____

Today I am *Grateful* for _____

_____

_____

_____

_____

_____

I love the LORD, because he hath heard my voice and my supplications.
Psalm 116:1, KJV

Day: _____ *Date:* ____ / ____ / ____

Today I am *Grateful* for _____

_____

_____

_____

_____

_____

Day: _____ *Date:* ____ / ____ / ____

Today I am *Grateful* for _____

_____

_____

_____

_____

_____

_____

I love them that love me; and those that seek me early shall find me. Proverbs 8:17, KJV

Day: _____ *Date:* ____ / ____ / ____

Today I am *Grateful* for _____

_____

_____

_____

_____

_____

Day: _____ *Date:* ____/ ____/ ____

Today I am *Grateful* for _____

_____

_____

_____

_____

_____

_____

And this I pray, that your love may abound yet more and more in knowledge and in all judgment; Philippians 1:9, KJV

Day: _____ *Date:* ____/ ____/ ____

Today I am *Grateful* for _____

_____

_____

_____

_____

_____

_____

Day: _____ *Date:* ____ / ____ / ____

Today I am *Grateful* for _____

_____

_____

_____

_____

_____

_____

Finally, be ye all of one mind, having compassion one of another, love as brethren, be pitiful, be courteous: 1 Peter 3:8, KJV

Day: _____ *Date:* ____ / ____ / ____

Today I am *Grateful* for _____

_____

_____

_____

_____

_____

_____

Day: _____ *Date:* ____/____/____

Today I am *Grateful* for _____

_____

_____

_____

_____

_____

_____

Jesus answered and said unto him, If a man love me, he will keep my words: and my Father will love him, and we will come unto him, and make our abode with him.
John 14:23, KJV

Day: _____ *Date:* ____/____/____

Today I am *Grateful* for _____

_____

_____

_____

_____

_____

_____

Day: _____ *Date:* ____/ ____/ ____

Today I am *Grateful* for _____

_____

_____

_____

_____

_____

_____

And we have known and believed the love that God hath to us. God is love; and he that dwelleth in love dwelleth in God, and God in him. 1 John 4:16, KJV

Day: _____ *Date:* ____/ ____/ ____

Today I am *Grateful* for _____

_____

_____

_____

_____

_____

_____

Day: _____ *Date:* ____ / ____ / ____

Today I am *Grateful* for _____

_____

_____

_____

_____

_____

_____

For this is the message that ye heard from the beginning, that we should love
one another. 1 John 3:11, KJV

Day: _____ *Date:* ____ / ____ / ____

Today I am *Grateful* for _____

_____

_____

_____

_____

_____

_____

Day: _____ *Date:* ____ / ____ / ____

Today I am *Grateful* for _____

_____

_____

_____

_____

_____

*Now the end of the commandment is charity out of a pure heart, and of a good conscience,
and of faith unfeigned: 1 Timothy 1:5, KJV*

Day: _____ *Date:* ____ / ____ / ____

Today I am *Grateful* for _____

_____

_____

_____

_____

_____

Day: _____ *Date:* ____ / ____ / ____

Today I am *Grateful* for _____

_____

_____

_____

_____

_____

_____

Beloved, if God so loved us, we ought also to love one another. 1 John 4:11, KJV

Day: _____ *Date:* ____ / ____ / ____

Today I am *Grateful* for _____

_____

_____

_____

_____

_____

_____

Day: _____ *Date:* ____/____/____

Today I am *Grateful* for _____

_____

_____

_____

_____

_____

_____

Fulfil ye my joy, that ye be likeminded, having the same love, being of one accord, of one mind. Philippians 2:2, KJV

Day: _____ *Date:* ____/____/____

Today I am *Grateful* for _____

_____

_____

_____

_____

_____

Day: _____ *Date:* _____ / _____ / _____

Today I am *Grateful* for _____

_____

_____

_____

_____

_____

_____

And be ye kind one to another, tenderhearted, forgiving one another, even as God for Christ's sake hath forgiven you. Ephesians 4:32, KJV

Day: _____ *Date:* _____ / _____ / _____

Today I am *Grateful* for _____

_____

_____

_____

_____

_____

_____

Day: _____ *Date:* ____/ ____/ ____

Today I am *Grateful* for _____

_____

_____

_____

_____

_____

Love not the world, neither the things that are in the world. If any man love the world, the love of the Father is not in him. 1 John 2:15, KJV

Day: _____ *Date:* ____/ ____/ ____

Today I am *Grateful* for _____

_____

_____

_____

_____

_____

Day: _____ *Date:* ____ / ____ / ____

Today I am *Grateful* for _____

_____

_____

_____

_____

_____

_____

Ask, and it shall be given you; seek, and ye shall find; knock, and it shall be opened unto you: Matthew 7:7, KJV

Day: _____ *Date:* ____ / ____ / ____

Today I am *Grateful* for _____

_____

_____

_____

_____

_____

Day: _____ *Date:* ___/___/___

Today I am *Grateful* for _____

_____

_____

_____

_____

_____

_____

And this commandment have we from him, That he who loveth God love his brother also.
1 John 4:21, KJV

Day: _____ *Date:* ___/___/___

Today I am *Grateful* for _____

_____

_____

_____

_____

_____

Printed in Great Britain
by Amazon

27570609R00067